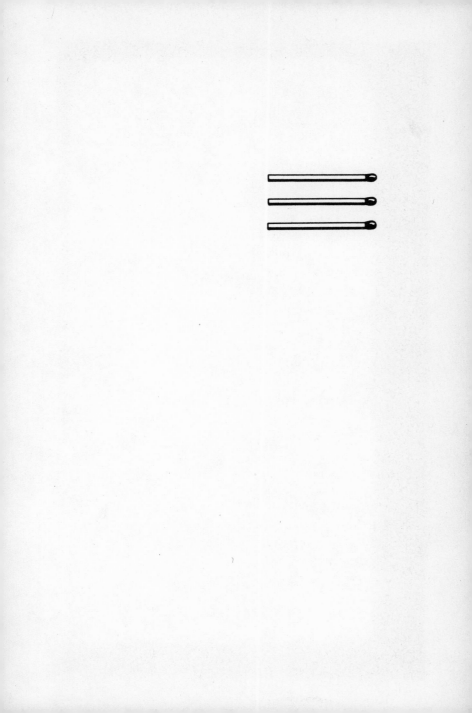

MATCHSTICK

PUZZLES, TRICKS & GAMES

By Gilbert Obermair

STERLING PUBLISHING CO., INC. NEW YORK

Oak Tree Press Co., Ltd. London & Sydney

3022480

OTHER BOOKS OF INTEREST

Calculator Puzzles, Tricks and Games   Eye Teasers
Code Games   Junior Magic

101 Best Magic Tricks

Hokus Pokus: Coin Tricks
Hokus Pokus: Rope & Scarf Tricks

Drawings by Holger Majoran
Translated by Manly Banister
Adapted by Louisa Bumagin Hellegers

Second Printing, 1978
Copyright © 1977 by Sterling Publishing Co., Inc.
Two Park Avenue, New York, N.Y. 10016
Distributed in Australia by Oak Tree Press Co., Ltd.,
P.O. Box J34, Brickfield Hill, Sydney 2000, N.S.W.
Distributed in the United Kingdom
by Ward Lock Ltd., 116 Baker Street, London W 1
Originally published in Germany under the title "Streichholz-Spielereien"
© 1975 by Wilhelm Heyne Verlag, Munich.
Manufactured in the United States of America
All rights reserved
Library of Congress Catalog Card No.: 77-79510
Sterling ISBN 0-8069-4564-8 Trade   Oak Tree 7061-2568-1
4565-6 Library

6.1.79 Pub. 4.99

Contents

R.3

1. Do You Have a Match?

Take a box of matches to start with. Have you ever reflected upon what a secret treasure you hold there in your hand? Scratch a match—and it lights. In less than one second and for a fraction of a penny.

Our ancestors did not have it so simple. They used two sticks, a great deal of exercise, and, above all, persistence. They had to rub the sticks together until the kindling temperature of the wood was reached. Then they had to take a piece of dry tinder from a tree, lay it on the hot, smoking sticks and blow on it until it caught fire. Variations of this method are still being used today by native tribes in Africa and South America. Sometimes it takes hours to obtain the desired result. What an agony for the fellow sitting by, waiting to light his pipe!

It was a long way from this first fire-maker to the use of a piece of flint to strike fire. With this, the spark that flew off set fire to the dry tinder. It was an even longer way through the development of various chemical fire lighters to that so-called "sulphur match" with its poisonous phosphorus head.

It was not until 1848 that the Frankfurt chemistry professor Rudolph Christian Boettger (1806–1881) invented what he called a "safety match" in which a non-dangerous red phosphorus match was scratched against a specially prepared striking surface. However, when nobody in Germany wanted anything to do with this invention, the rights were bought up by a Swede and further developed in the next seven years by J. E. Lundström, who invented the safety match as we know it and at the same time first made the telescoping box to contain them. By 1903, the dangerous phosphorus matches were forbidden and Boettger's and Lundström's safety matches began their victory march around the world known as "Swedish matches." Not only were safety matches a better and less expensive way of making fire, but also the little matchbox provided a box for games, as we shall see in this book.

The first thing to do before trying out any of the puzzles in this book is to light all the matches, one by one, and blow them out quickly. Now you have a number of matchsticks with burnt heads which cannot go off and burn you when you are playing with them.

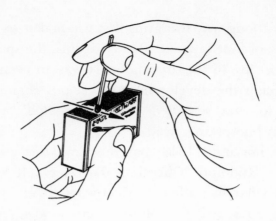

To light a match, you should not strike it down the length of the striking surface (on the box). Trixor the magician has convinced me that by doing so, you wear out the striking surfaces very quickly. It suffices to strike the match across the width of the striking surface.

Now, get ready—the fun begins!

2. Word Games

Strangely, many serious people have the most fun playing matchstick games. This is because solving the problems involves *thinking*. But, surely this adds to the fun you can have with these enjoyable puzzles and tricks which, like so many old jokes, get passed on by word of mouth—or rather by movement of hand!

Before we begin, note that the problems, whose solutions you will find at the back of the book, are *not* given here in continuous numerical order. Otherwise, when you look up a solution, the solution to the next problem would be staring you in the eye.

Now, turn the page and start with a very simple game.

The Happy Pig

The picture here shows a sad pig, made up of 15½ matchsticks. See if you can turn it into a happy pig by simply changing the position of 3½ matchsticks.

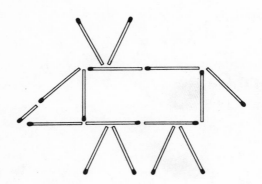

See solution 149.

Do you have the idea? Now, let's begin with some simple word games.

The Secret Beloved

Joan is the daughter of a sly old magician. Lay out her lovely name on the table using 13 matchsticks.

Now move 5 matchsticks, and see if you can spell the name of her secret beloved.

See solution 97.

Discover Words

This time, make 4 figures as shown in the drawing. Then try to construct words from the shapes by removing 8, 9, 10, 11, 12 and 13 matchsticks.

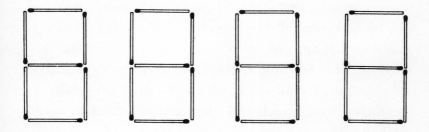

See solution 1.

This is also a fun game to play with several people. Each player lays out a basic figure and then tries to create words by subtracting a set number of matchsticks. The first person to find 6 words wins.

3. Calculus Lectures

Recently, a group of friends got together to play word games with matchsticks. Calculus the mathematician sat by and sneered. He suddenly asked us if we knew of anything significant to pursue with matchsticks. For example, he asked, could we use them to expand our knowledge of mathematics? He referred especially to geometry, which deals with the types of shapes we could make from matchsticks.

And he soon began, with slender fingers, to lay out figures and to explain their peculiarities. The following is a simplified explanation of what he said.

A quadrangle, he explained, is a figure with four corners connected by four sides. It doesn't matter whether two of the sides—or two sets of two—are parallel, whether two, three, or four of the sides are equal in length, or whether the angles are:

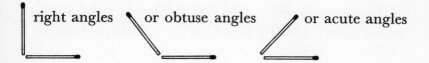

right angles   or obtuse angles   or acute angles

For example, the figure shown here is a quadrangle with different length sides, no two of which are parallel, and which does not have any right angles, but two obtuse and two acute angles.

This quadrangle figure, called a *trapezoid*, has two parallel sides.

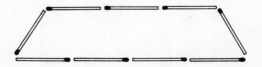

This quadrangle, a *deltoid*, has two sets of sides of equal length which have equal angles between them.

Shown here is a *parallelogram*, which consists of two pairs of parallel sides. A parallelogram is also a quadrangle.

One type of parallelogram has *one* right angle, which means, therefore, that it must have *four* right angles. This special parallelogram is called a *rectangle*. A rectangle is thus a parallelogram and a quadrangle.

Some rectangles have all four sides the same length. This special form of rectangle is called a *square*. A square is thus a rectangle and a parallelogram and a quadrangle. Moreover, a square is naturally also a trapezoid because it has two parallel sides. A square is also a deltoid, because it has two pairs of two sides of equal length with equal angles between them.

A parallelogram with sides of equal length is also a *rhombus* or *diamond*

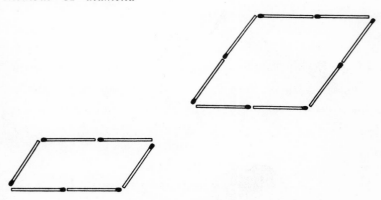

and one with unequal sides is a *rhomboid*. Both can but do not have to be rectangular.

A rectangular rhomboid is a parallelogram and a rectangle and a trapezoid and a quadrangle. A rectangular rhombus is also a square. A square is also a rhomboid.

When you have understood Calculus the mathematician and have these shapes and their names sorted out in your head, it's then time for some matchstick problems.

What kind of a figure is this? Several answers can be correct.

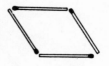

a: a square
b: a diamond
c: a trapezoid
d: a rhomboid
e: a deltoid

See solution 2.

And this one?

a: a quadrangle
b: a rectangle
c: a rhombus
d: a rhomboid
e: a square

See solution 113.

And this one?

a: a square
b: a diamond
c: a trapezoid
d: a rhomboid
e: a deltoid

See solution 68.

17

4. About Squares

The teachings of Calculus stirred our imaginations. Each of us suddenly thought of a puzzle which involved squares or rectangles. Following are some of the best problems we created.

Start with this matchstick figure in which 12 matchsticks make 5 squares—1 big and 4 small.

Remove 2 matchsticks to make 2 squares.
See solution 3.

Now move 4 matchsticks to make 2 squares.
See solution 36.
Move 4 matchsticks to make 3 squares.
See solution 14.
Move 3 matchsticks to make 3 squares.
See solution 65.
Move 2 matchsticks to make 3 big and 4 small squares.
See solution 118.
Move 2 matchsticks to make 3 squares, 4 small rectangles, and 4 big rectangles.
See solution 140.
Add 4 matchsticks to make 5 more squares!
See solution 6.

Now use 12 matchsticks to lay out the following figure:

Move 3 matchsticks to make 3 squares.
See solution 12.
Move 4 matchsticks to make a cross.
See solution 18.

Here is another figure to work with:

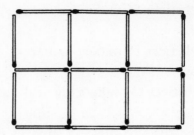

Remove 5 matchsticks, so that 3 squares remain.
See solution 4.
Remove 6 matchsticks, so that 2 squares remain.
See solution 15.

The following problems are quite similar:

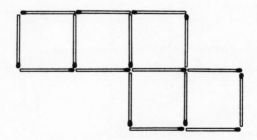

Move 4 matchsticks to make 6 squares.
See solution 110.

Move 2 matchsticks to make 4 equal-sized squares.
See solution 85.

Move 2 matchsticks to make 4 squares—3 small and one large.
See solution 142.

For the next group of problems, use 22 matchsticks to lay out the basic pattern shown here:

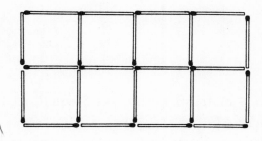

Remove 10 matchsticks to make 4 squares.
See solution 99.

Remove 9 matchsticks to make 4 squares.
See solution 119.

Remove 8 matchsticks to make 4 squares.
See solution 127.

Remove 7 matchsticks to make 4 squares.
See solution 143.

Remove 6 matchsticks to make 4 squares.
See solution 9.

Remove 5 matchsticks to make 4 squares.
See solution 16.

Here's a real brain teaser. Lay out 24 matchsticks to form a 9-square grid and try the following problems using that basic figure.

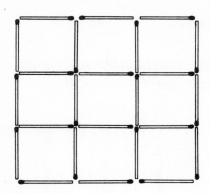

Remove 4 matchsticks to make 5 equal-sized squares.
See solution 13.

Remove 4 matchsticks to make 1 large and 4 small squares.
See solution 29.

Remove 4 matchsticks to make 6 squares.
See solution 70.

Remove 4 matchsticks to make 9 squares.
See solution 83.

Remove 6 matchsticks to make 3 different-sized squares.
See solution 90.

Remove 6 matchsticks to make 3 different-sized squares and 2 rectangles.
See solution 71.

Remove 8 matchsticks to make 2 same-sized and 1 small square.
See solution 117.

Remove 8 matchsticks to make 2 different-sized squares (2 solutions).
See solution 134.

Remove 8 matchsticks to make 4 squares.
See solution 125.

Move 8 matchsticks to make 3 different-sized squares.
See solution 147.

Remove 12 matchsticks to make 3 squares.
See solution 14.

Move 12 matchsticks to make 2 same-sized squares.
See solution 146.

Here is a similar problem. Use 15 matchsticks to make a spiral-like figure like the one shown:

Move 3 matchsticks to make 2 squares.
See solution 94.

Construct a building from 11 matchsticks:

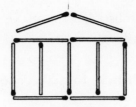

Move 4 matchsticks to make 11 squares.
See solution 38.
Move 2 matchsticks to make 11 squares.
See solution 116.

Lay out 5 squares using 16 matchsticks:

Move 6 matchsticks to make 4 squares.
See solution 104.
Move 4 matchsticks to make 4 squares.
See solution 43.

The following figure consists of 3 quadrangles:

Take away 1 matchstick and try to construct 3 different quadrangles from the remaining matchsticks. It works!

See solution 128.

Calculus Special

The most interesting problem came from Calculus himself. Carefully, he laid 4 matchsticks on the table. And then came the problem: Move just *one* matchstick, so that *one* square results.

Calculus thought that this problem could be solved either by intuitive thinking or by persistent thinking. In intuitive thinking, the steps leading to the solution would not all be visible. Instead, the solution could be reached by a sudden intuitive leap of the mind. The result would depend more on hitting upon the right answer than by carefully reasoning out an answer. In persistent thinking, the solution would result from a progressive sequence of steps. This sequence would not necessarily have to be in any kind of logical sequence, but the steps in this method would follow one after the other.

Then Calculus explained that the experience we gained working out the previous problem involving squares could actually delay our finding the solution to this one, or even prevent finding it altogether! What did he mean by that? At any rate, we were ready to bet this problem was unsolvable. What do *you* think?

See solution 44.

5. About Triangles

A triangle is a figure composed of three points not lying in a straight line and the connecting lines between these points. The sum of two sides is always greater than the third side. The largest angle always lies opposite the longest side, and the smallest angle always lies opposite the shortest side.

There are obtuse or scalene triangles, in which the sides are unequal in length, isosceles triangles, which

obtuse triangle

isosceles triangle

have two sides equal in length, and equilateral triangles, which have all three sides equal in length.

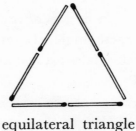

equilateral triangle

An unequal-sided triangle and an isosceles triangle can also be right triangles, which means that one of the three angles is a right angle. An equilateral triangle, however, can never be a right triangle because each of its angles is 60°.

You can, however, make two right triangles out of any triangle, says Calculus, including an equilateral triangle, by dividing the triangle with a straight line which drops perpendicularly from one point to the opposite line as shown in the drawing.

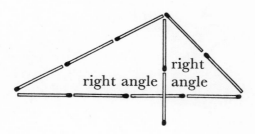

right angle | right angle

The right triangle has a unique trait. Thousands of years ago, the Babylonians developed geometry which they used to help them build dams and to calculate measures. They also set up a theorem, which was later ascribed to the Greek, Pythagoras: the square of the hypotenuse (the longest side in a right triangle) is equal to the sum of the squares of the other two sides.

To prove this, make a right triangle whose sides have the smallest possible whole number of lines—a = 3, b = 4 and c = 5 matchsticks. Then construct a square of matchsticks from each side of this right triangle.

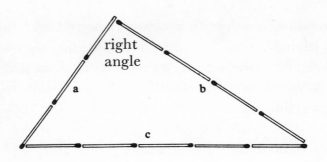

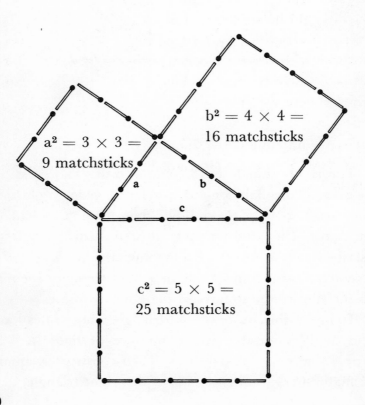

Now add $a^2 + b^2 = c^2$, and you can see that, indeed, $9 + 16 = 25$.

This knowledge benefitted the Babylonians and the Egyptians. After each annual flooding of the Nile, the Egyptians had to survey the land by the river. For this, they used a 12-unit-long knotted rope which was marked into divisions of 3, 4 and 5 units. The rope was then straightened out by a so-called "rope stretcher" until the markings lay on the angles of a triangle. The resulting triangle was a right triangle, and with it, right angles could be constructed anywhere in the land.

Calculus took a deep breath, but before he could continue with his dissertation, his listeners instinctively began to solve triangle problems. The most interesting of these were the following:

Here is an equilateral triangle. Add 3 matchsticks to it so that 5 equilateral triangles result—4 small and 1 large.

See solution 7.

Here are 3 equilateral triangles. Move 2 matchsticks to make 4 equilateral triangles.

See solution 31.

With 5 matchsticks, construct 2 isosceles triangles which have only 1 point in common.
See solution 37.

With 4 matchsticks, construct 2 isosceles triangles which have only 1 point in common.
See solution 108.

Construct the figure shown below on a table using 12 matchsticks. Now move 4 matchsticks so that 6 equilateral triangles result.

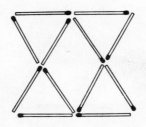

See solution 10.

How many triangles are contained in this figure?

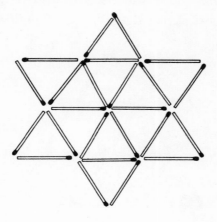

See solution 24.

Using 8 matchsticks, make 4 right triangles the same size and 2 squares of different size.
See solution 69.

Make a tomahawk with 9 matchsticks. Move 5 matchsticks so that 5 triangles result.

See solution 19.

Using 18 matchsticks, construct 13 equilateral triangles—9 small, 3 middle-sized, and 1 large. Take away 5 matchsticks so that only 5 triangles remain.

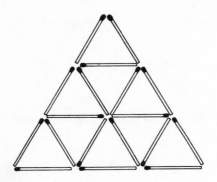

See solution 59.

Build a small house with 6 matchsticks. Move 3 matchsticks around so that 4 equilateral triangles result.

See solution 72.

And now, with the same 6 matchsticks construct 12 right triangles.

See solution 39.

Calculus Special

Again, Calculus had the last word. Lost in thought, he took the 6 matchsticks into his hand. "Let's try once more," he said, "to construct 4 equilateral triangles with them—similar to the next to last problem we did. However, this time, each side of this triangle is to be only *one* matchstick long.

"Again, it is possible that our experiences with the previous problems may delay or prevent our finding the correct solution. Is this problem solvable?"

What do *you* think?

See solution 122.

6. About Rhombuses and Rhomboids

Do you remember from page 13 what a rhombus is? It is also called a lozenge (it looks like a pushed-out-of-shape square). Remember, too, that a rhomboid is a pushed-out-of-shape rectangle (a parallelogram).

Let's see if we can solve some interesting problems involving these figures. I hope we do not have to disturb Calculus again.

Move these 3 E's so that 6 rhomboids, 3 rhombuses and 1 hexagon result.

See solution 66.

Lay out a star with 18 matchsticks. Change the positions of 6 matchsticks so that the star contains 6 equal-sized rhombuses.

See solution 22.

Change the positions of 2 matchsticks in the figure below to create 4 rhomboids and 2 rhombuses.

See solution 11.

Again change the positions of 2 matchsticks in the basic figure above to make 3 rhombuses and 4 triangles.

See solution 17.

Change the positions of 4 matchsticks in the figure below to make 2 rhombuses and 5 rhomboids.

See solution 100.

Move 5 matchsticks to make 3 rhombuses.

See solution 128.

Change positions of 4 matchsticks in the new figure created above to make 5 triangles.
See solution 129.

Take 3 matchsticks away from the figure below so as to leave 6 triangles in 3 rhombuses.

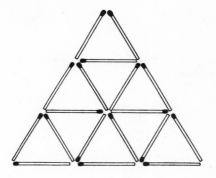

See solution 20.

Take 5 matchsticks away from the same figure to make 2 rhombuses and 5 triangles.
See solution 28.

Move 2 matchsticks and add 1 to the figure below to make 2 rhombuses.

See solution 77.

In the star below, move 6 matchsticks to make 3 rhombuses.

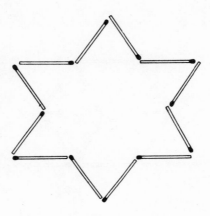

See solution 92.

And now, with 12 matchsticks, lay out a basic figure to serve as a start for the 6 problems below. The figure is a hexagon (6-sided figure) enclosing 6 equilateral triangles.

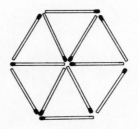

Move 4 matchsticks to make 5 rhombuses—1 large and 4 small.
See solution 40.

Move 3 matchsticks to make 4 rhombuses.
See solution 49.

Move 2 matchsticks to make 6 triangles—5 small and 1 large.
See solution 95.

Move 3 matchsticks to make 3 rhombuses and 6 rhomboids.
See solution 66.

Move 4 matchsticks to make 1 rhombus and 3 hexagons—2 small and 1 large.
See solution 58.

Move 3 matchsticks to make 4 triangles.
See solution 82.

7. A Visit with a Shepherd

After so much concentration and thinking, we decided a walk would certainly do us some good. So, we hiked out into the country to visit Nicodemus, the old shepherd, and his flock. To be sure, he doesn't talk a lot, but he surely is a sly fox, true to his motto: "He who is stupid is eaten by the wolves."

We were lucky that day—he was very sociable. Following are some of his tales.

This problem was already known in the Middle Ages. A shepherd had 10 fences. One day he had to tend twice as many sheep. He added 2 fences and suddenly had twice as much room for his animals. How were the fences set up before and after?

See solution 121.

Another shepherd had 26 fences. One day, when he had 3 times as many sheep to tend, he took away 2 fences and moved the remainder around so that he had 3 times as much room for his animals. How were the fences set up before and after?

See solution 107.

A farmer had 8 nanny goats and surrounded each one with 4 of his 25 fences. One night, 3 fences were stolen, but no goats. The farmer then moved the fences around and once again each goat had a pen to herself. How did he do it?

See solution 78.

How many fences could the farmer do without and still enclose each goat alone? And then how would the pen look?

See solution 132.

Then Nicodemus, too, presented a difficult problem. His flock usually grazed between 4 trees and he had enclosed the area in a square consisting of 8 fences. Then he wanted to more than double the grazing area. He wanted it to still be square and still be contained within the area of the same 4 trees. How did he solve the problem and how many fences did he need for it?

See solution 25.

A farmer set up 38 sections of fence and kept his sheep in this pen. One day, 2 fences were lost and the number of sheep greatly increased. The farmer had to reconstruct the fences so as to enclose an area which was:

1½ times *(see solution 32)*
2½ times *(see solution 52)*
3½ times *(see solution 67)*
4½ times *(see solution 80)*
as big an area
as that of the
original figure.

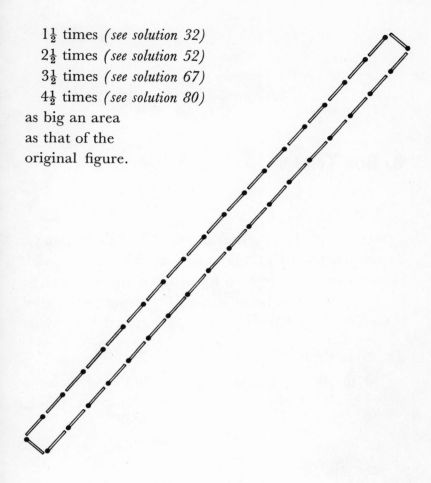

What shape did these 4 pens have?

8. Box Tricks

When Calculus celebrated his children's birthdays, Trixor the magician, who was a friend of the family, came to visit. He enjoyed himself helping the children have fun with matchstick games. Following are some of the games they played at the party. First they tried:

The Nose Relay

The players sat around a table. One player took the sleeve of a matchbox and placed it on his nose. Then,

the player on his or her left had to take the sleeve off the first player's nose without using his or her hands.

So it went around the table, moving from nose to nose. Anyone who let the box fall had to pay a forfeit.

A Guessing Game

Then followed a guessing game. Without showing how many, the leader of the game put a few matchsticks in the box and closed it. Each player had to shake the box and try to guess how many matchsticks were in it. Whoever guessed correctly was given the matchsticks. The box was then filled again for another try.

The Unbreakable Matchbox

The unbreakable matchbox came along next. The sleeve of the box was set on the table with one of its

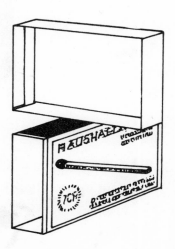

striking surfaces down. The drawer was stood on edge on the other striking surface. Each player tried to smash the box with a powerful blow of the fist, but never succeeded! Each time the pressure of the fist was transmitted to the sleeve, it immediately turned to one side.

The Matchstick Lift

This trick was performed by Calculus himself. He separated the sleeve and drawer from each other and laid them on a table, both with the open sides up. Between them he placed several matchsticks, side by side.

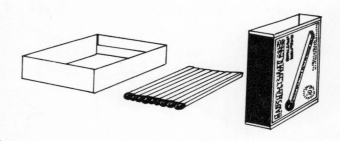

The object was, without using hands, to transfer all the matchsticks at one time into the drawer. Can you do it?

See solution 5.

9. Matchstick Magic

Then it was time for Trixor the magician to entertain the little audience with some of his magic tricks. When I asked him if he would explain his tricks afterwards, he murmured, "The greatest magic lies in secrecy," for he did not wish to reveal anything about his matchbox tricks. Not until he heard that it was for this book did he open up. Promise that you will reveal to no one the secrets of Trixor's tricks; otherwise you will ruin some beautiful illusions and a lot of fun for future viewers. Ready now? Here comes Trixor's magic.

Hypnosis

Trixor laid a matchbox on the table and asserted that he could, by means of hypnosis, make the children do whatever he wished. He took 10 matchsticks out of the box and constructed two little piles with them, the first containing 3 and the second 7 matchsticks. Then he asked little Peter to quickly put the tip of his finger on one of the piles. Peter placed the tip of his finger on the pile containing 3 matchsticks and Trixor said, "I knew you would do that!"

He turned the box over and on the bottom of the box was written:

How did he know?
See solution 21.

Trixor himself narrated the next trick.

Gravity

"I take a matchstick out of the box, hold it over the table and let it go—what happens? It falls downwards, for it obeys the natural law of gravity. However, when I touch the box with my magic wand, this law is no longer valid for the matchsticks. For 3 magical seconds,

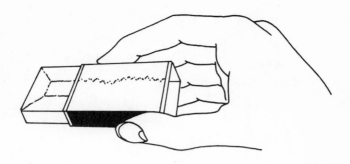

this law will be contradicted. Please, watch: I turn the box over, open it and—nothing falls out.

"You think that the box may be empty? No, it is not. I take out a matchstick. Here is the box, with many matchsticks still in it. You can check for yourself."

What was Trixor's secret?

See solution 30.

The Disappearing Matchbox

The magician pulled out a handkerchief and laid it beside a matchbox. He explained that it was a magic handkerchief which possessed magical powers. Then he took the box in his left hand, covered it with the handkerchief and asked one of the small viewers to hold the

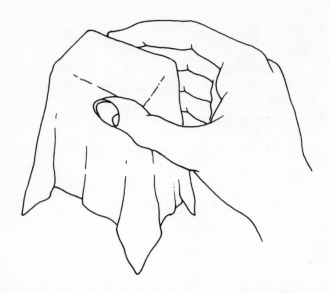

covered box firmly through the handkerchief. At the count of 3, the child was to let the box go again.

Trixor took hold of a corner of the handkerchief and counted, "1—2—3." At the count of "3," the child let go and the magician pulled the handkerchief away. The matchbox had disappeared and had landed in Trixor's trousers pocket! How did that happen?

See solution 46.

Penetration

Trixor showed a matchbox. The drawer was half open so the audience could see that it was empty. A coin lay on the table.

The magician closed the box and placed it on top of the coin. He said the magic word—"abracadabra"—and the coin turned up inside the drawer! How?

See solution 64.

Illusion

The great magician then took a matchbox out of his trousers pocket, placed it on the back of his hand, muttered some magic words, and the box came to life. It actually moved slowly down the back of his hand towards him.

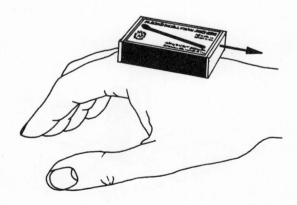

Then he turned his hand over so that his palm faced up and he placed the box on his wrist. Again he said some magic words and the matchbox moved in the opposite direction, towards his fingertips.

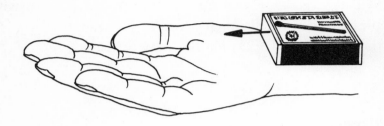

Next, the magician placed the box on his palm and held it firmly against the base of his fingers. Again he uttered some secret words and the box slowly opened itself until the matchsticks inside were visible.

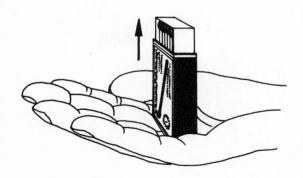

How did Trixor accomplish these magic feats?
See solution 74.

The Obedient Box

Trixor opened an empty matchbox and, with a knife, bored a hole in each of the narrow ends of the drawer. He then pulled a thread through the holes and put the drawer in its sleeve.

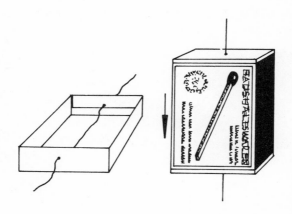

With both hands, he held up one end of the thread so that the other end hung down. Then he gave the box instructions. Every time he said, "Down!", the box was to slip downwards and every time he said, "Stop!", it was to stop immediately.

After Trixor's demonstration, the children all checked the box and thread and even tried out the trick. They just could not make it work—the box slipped from the top all the way to the bottom of the thread. The children were astonished, because everything took place right in front of their noses. They had watched like hawks, but they had been unable to find an explanation for the trick.

"It goes without saying that there *is* a little trick to it," said Trixor modestly. "However, it is not enough just to know the trick to be able to perform it. From knowing to doing is a big step. Practice makes perfect." Can you figure it out?

See solution 35.

10. Micromagic

"Even small things can delight us," said Trixor the magician. By this he referred to "micromagic"—sorcery at the table, in a small group, using small, everyday things such as knives, spoons, napkins or handkerchiefs, and matchsticks. To the unsophisticated viewer, a coin which penetrates inside a glass is as great a miracle as a magician's assistant being sawed in two on the stage. The charm lies in the fact that the viewer is sitting right beside the magician, but still cannot explain the marvel being performed. In micromagic, there is no special lighting as there is on the stage, no trapdoors, no stage wings and no assistants. Here sits a person—the magician —alone with his or her skilful hands.

Do not think, however, that you can perform micromagic without practice. Just as in stage magic, every trick has to be carefully thought through and thoroughly studied—not until then can you achieve the intended effect.

Try to "sell" your tricks as efficiently as possible. Be sure you have plenty of time and don't have to hurry. Surround each trick with a number of little stories. And what's more, don't betray the secrets! Especially, never perform the same trick twice in a row. If you follow these bits of advice, you will no doubt succeed in astonishing your audience.

Somersault

Lay a matchbox at the edge of a table. From it, take a matchstick and lay it with its head on the box and half its length hanging over the box and the table's edge. To perform the magic, carefully touch the first matchstick with a second and—"abracadabra"—the first matchstick somersaults. What do you think? No, no. The magician's hands are completely motionless at the time.

See solution 105.

The Indian Cloth

Trixor next showed us a silk cloth which, he said, was given to him by an Indian fakir as a gift. It has quite unusual properties.

He asked one viewer to take a match from the table and place it in the cloth. With magnetic stroking and by blowing on it with his magical breath, Trixor awakened the mystic powers in the cloth. Then he folded the cloth inwards over the matchstick, and turned it around. He asked his assistant to take hold of the matchstick through the cloth and break it.

The cloth then had the problem of repairing the damage. Trixor blew on the cloth, shook—and "abra-cadabra"—the match fell out unbroken.

How? No. The cloth was empty. It had no seams, either, in which a second matchstick was hidden.

See solution 76.

The Magic Eleven

The magician placed 19 matchsticks on the table and posed the problem—to make 11 out of them, without breaking a matchstick or adding any matches to the original number.

Here's how he did it:

Then he took away 15 matchsticks, so that only 4 remained on the table, and he again posed the same problem—that is, make 11 from these also.

Now he removed 1 more matchstick. Out of the remaining 3 matchsticks, can you figure out how he made 11 again?

Lastly, the magician took away 2 more matchsticks, so that only a single one remained on the table. How did he make 11 out of that? It was a small and simple thing for the magician.

See solution 84.

The Magnetic Matchsticks

"Certainly," said Trixor, "you are familiar with the principles of magnetism. Every bar magnet, for example, has 2 poles, 1 positive and the other negative. If you bring another magnet close to the first one, you will see that the 2 poles either attract or repel each other.

"Let's try this out. Unfortunately, I do not have a magnet on hand. For better or worse, I must make do with my matchbox. Let's say that these 2 matchsticks represent magnets. By merely blowing on them, I can awaken in them special physical properties.

"In order to have a foundation, I lay a third matchstick lengthwise on top of the box. On this matchstick, I carefully lay the first magnet so that it is balanced horizontally on the foundation matchstick.

"Hopefully, the magnetism reaches out so that I can demonstrate to you what I explained above. To help me,

I rub the second magnet on the sleeve of my jacket. As you know, rubbing generates heat, electricity, and in this case, also magnetism.

"I now place the second matchstick magnet on the front right quarter of the box.

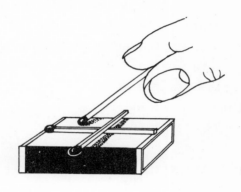

"Did you see it? The first magnet quickly turned itself towards the second and now it is sticking to it. Quite by accident, I found 2 similar and attracting poles. And now, let us try the opposite. First, I place the first magnet in its original position. Then I rub the second on my sleeve and place it in the front left quarter of the box. You see—the poles repel each other."

How did Trixor make his matchsticks magnetic?
See solution 96.

The Bewitched Matchstick

Trixor opened the matchbox and took out one of the matchsticks to show the audience. He shook the matchbox to show it still contained a few matchsticks. These were to become bewitched.

Trixor then closed the box, blew on the top of the matchbox sleeve, pulled out the drawer, and—"abracadabra"—the box was empty! He even pulled the drawer all the way out and showed it around.

Then he closed the box again and rubbed it between his hands. "Abracadabra!" When he opened the box, the matchsticks were in it again.

Can you perform *this* magic?
See solution 98.

Penetration of Matter

The magician brought out a safety pin on which he had skewered a matchstick. He then snapped his middle finger against the matchstick—whose head had been broken off, of course—and it visibly passed through the shank of the pin. How?

See solution 102.

The Stingy Matchbox

"May I ask you for a match?"

"Well, now! The drawer slid shut by itself!"

How did that happen?

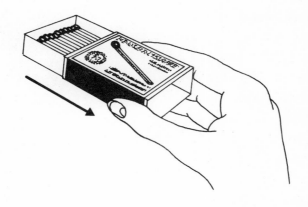

See solution 144.

The Puzzling Dots

The magician held 2 flat matchsticks in his hands. He held 1 between the thumb and forefinger of his left hand and the other the same way in his right. He showed both sides of the matchsticks—each had 2 clean surfaces.

Then, with the ring finger of his left hand, he stroked the right matchstick, blew on it, and, on the previously clean surface, a black dot appeared. Then he turned the right matchstick over to show the other side—a black dot also appeared there.

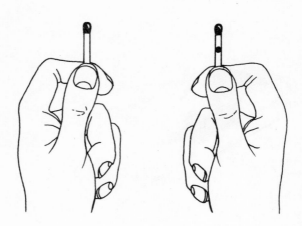

Next, he passed the ring finger of his right hand over the left matchstick and blew on it: the dot disappeared from the right matchstick and appeared on the left. Then he showed both sides of the matchsticks. The right matchstick was clean on both sides, but the dot was now also on the second surface of the left matchstick.

Again, the magician moved his hands towards each other—the dots again appeared on the right matchstick. With still another movement—"abracadabra"—the flat surfaces of both matchsticks were clean.

What happened?

See solution 123.

Into Nothing

Trixor put 3 matchsticks on the table. He wanted to dissolve them into nothing before our very eyes! He asked a member of the audience to stretch out her left hand in such a way that the palm was turned towards the magician. He asked this assistant to clench her fingers, leaving only her thumb outspread.

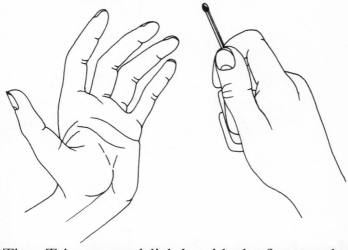

Then Trixor tapped lightly with the first matchstick in the space between the thumb and forefinger of his helper's hand. At the third touch, the helper was to try to grab hold of the matchstick firmly with her thumb.

1—2—3! The matchstick vanished!

1—2—3! The second vanished too!

1—2—3! The third also dissolved into nothing. How can this be?

See solution 126.

The Magnetic Hair

"Even my hair is magnetic," claimed the magician. He pulled a hair out of his head and brought it close to 2 matchsticks he held in his other hand. Every time he brought the hair close to the matchsticks, they moved apart.

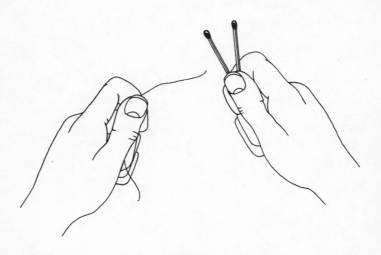

Of course, he allowed both the hair and the matchsticks to be examined by the audience. Can you explain this bit of magnetism?

See solution 130.

The Obedient Matchsticks

The great magician placed a bowl of water on the table and put 6 matchsticks on the surface of the water so that they formed a star. He then touched the water with his magic wand and—"abracadabra"—the matchsticks floated from the middle of the bowl to the sides.

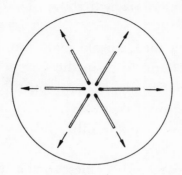

When he touched the water with his wand again— "abracadabra"—the obedient matchsticks gravitated back to the middle of the bowl.

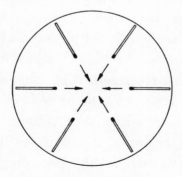

Can you explain this magic movement?
See solution 139.

The Old Magician

To end his micromagical show, Trixor told us this story:

"Once upon a time, an old magician, famed far and wide for his wisdom, lived in the Orient. When he felt that he was about to die, he summoned his 2 sons to his deathbed. He showed them 2 chests (matchboxes), 1 of which was empty, but the other filled with many gold pieces (matchsticks).

"Then he turned to his eldest son (a spectator), gave him the full chest and said: 'You are the eldest and so you have the first choice. I no longer know how many gold pieces are in the chest. Take out as many as you want, but fewer than 30 and no less than 20. Then give the chest with the remaining gold pieces to your younger brother (another spectator). Here, my elder son, is the empty chest. Place your gold pieces inside it.'

"However, the old magician understood people and he understood his elder son. And, therefore, he said to him: 'I do not know how many gold pieces you took, but now I ask you to give your younger brother a few more—as many as the second digit in the number you took, and again as many as the first digit (for instance, if the elder son had taken 27 gold pieces, he now had to give his younger brother 7 +2).

"When that was done, the old man died and his sons

could not rest until they had counted their inheritance (both sons count their gold pieces).

"And now you see the final wonder performed by the old magician. Both sons received the same number of gold pieces!"

Are you wise enough to figure out the secret?
See solution 148.

We close this chapter on micromagic with hearty applause for Trixor.

11. Thinking Division and Dividing Thoughts

In trying to solve the following two-part problems, you can proceed either intuitively (by trial and error) or logically (step by step).

A father bequeathed to his 4 sons a piece of land upon which stand 4 trees. Each son is to receive an equal share

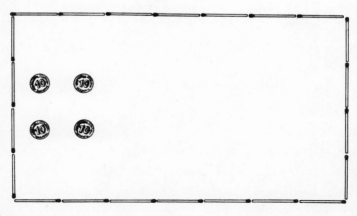

of the land as well as 1 of the trees. How should the sons divide the land without moving the trees?

See solution 8.

Another father also bequeathed to his 4 sons a piece of land with 4 trees. Each son is to receive a piece of land equal in area and of the same shape, as well as a tree. How should this piece of land be divided?

See solution 47.

Next is a division problem which you can solve only by logical and not by intuitive thinking. And what is more, you can also start with the desired conclusion and reconstruct the problem backwards from the end, step by step, until you have developed the beginning.

The Joseph Game

This ancient counting game goes back to the historian and military general Flavius Josephus. Hans Sachs, shoemaker and poet, also put the story into verse: "The XV Christians and XV Turks, who were travelling by sea. . . ."

How does it go? Fifteen people in party A and 15 people in party B are sailing the sea when their ship gets caught up in a storm. In order to keep the ship from sinking, half the travellers have to be thrown overboard. This is to take place in accordance with a certain ritual.

All 30 stand in a row. Beginning at the left, the passengers are counted off to 9 and this ninth person has to go overboard. Then, 9 more are counted off, and so on. When the end of the row is reached, the counting returns to the beginning of the line and continues.

The question is: How must the members of party A be arranged to ensure that only the travellers of party B have to jump overboard?

Indicate the members of party A by matchsticks laid with their heads up and of party B by matchsticks laid head down.

See solution 114.

Here is still another division problem whose solution requires logical thinking and testing.

Two treasure hunters found 10 gold pieces and 11 silver spoons. The smarter of the 2 proposed a special method of division, and laid out the gold pieces and silver spoons in a circle as shown. He then began count-

ing 10 times clockwise to 5, taking away an object at each count of 5. Next, the stupider hunter counted 11 times to 5, taking away 11 objects. Where did the smarter hunter start counting in order to get all 10 of the gold pieces?

See solution 81.

Strategy is very important in solving the following problems. In each case, you must choose the one step, from several possibilities, that is most suitable to help you win the game. To win, you must comprehend the situation more exactly—and quicker—than your opponent and deduce logical and valid strategies. If you are careful to do this, you should be able to play the following games well. Using incorrect strategies or your intuition could lead to your defeat!

From a small pile of 11 matchsticks, let 2 players, taking turns, remove from 1 to 3 matchsticks at a time. Whoever has to take the last matchstick loses. Who always wins?
See solution 27.

Lay 15 matchsticks on a table. Taking turns, 2 players remove 1 to 3 matchsticks at a time. Whoever has to take the last matchstick loses. How can one never lose?
See solution 33.

Lay 25 matchsticks on a table. Taking turns, each of 2 players removes 1 to 4 matchsticks at a time. Whoever takes away the last matchstick loses. Whoever goes first can direct the game so that he or she always wins. What happens if he or she must start second?
See solution 57.

Place 30 matchsticks in a pile. Taking turns, have 2 players remove 1 to 6 matchsticks at a time. The winner is the one who takes the last matchstick from the table. How does one win?

See solution 101.

Make 3 piles, each containing any number of matchsticks. The first player may take from one of the piles as many matchsticks as desired—even all of them. Whoever takes the last matchstick from the table loses. How can one win the game?

See solution 131.

To conclude this chapter, here is another division problem. In order to solve it, it is not sufficient to think intuitively, logically or strategically—there is a little trick to it. You must find out what it is.

Dividing the Camels

Ali Baba wants to divide 39 camels among his 4 sons. The first is to get half of them, the second a fourth, the third an eighth and the fourth a tenth. How can he solve the problem? Use matchsticks for the 39 camels.

Not until wise Ibrahim comes riding up to help can he do it. Why?

See solution 152.

12. The Ancient Romans

You are certainly familiar with Roman numerals. And, you must realize that you can easily represent the individual numerals using matchsticks. You probably

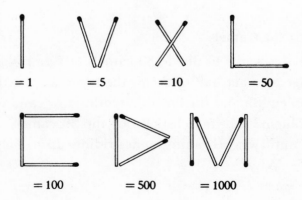

= 1   = 5   = 10   = 50

= 100   = 500   = 1000

also know that at the most, there can only be three similar figures written one after the other, which you add together to designate a number. One smaller figure may stand in front of a larger figure, which means you subtract its value from the larger figure. You can also write smaller figures after larger ones, and then add the values together. Thus, for example, these mean:

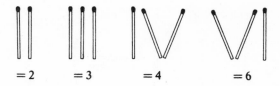

= 2   = 3   = 4   = 6

So, how can you make 4 or 6 out of 3 matchsticks? Correct. The solution is in the drawing above.

Let's suppose that the ancient Romans were acquainted with matchsticks. Then, how would they have written the following numbers (with matchsticks)?
8, 9, 24, 40, 78, 97, 99, 1975.
See solution 61.

From 19, take away a matchstick so that 20 remains.
See solution 23.

Lay 5 matchsticks on the table and take away 8, so that nothing remains.

See solution 48.

How can 3 dozen be made out of $\frac{3}{4}$ dozen?
See solution 141.

Add 1 matchstick to the following equation so that both sides of the equation are equal. There are 2 solutions.

See solution 111.

Here is another equation, the two sides of which are not equal. Make them equal by changing the position of 1 matchstick.

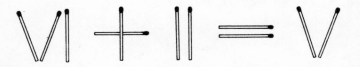

See solution 145.

Change the positions of 2 matchsticks so that both sides of this equation are equal.

$$X + X = X$$

See solution 88.

Change the position of 1 matchstick so both sides of the equation are equal. There are 2 solutions.

$$VI - IV = IX$$

See solution 124.

Move 1 matchstick so both sides of this equation are equal.

See solution 93.

Move 1 matchstick so both sides of this equation are equal.

See solution 91.

Prove that half of 12 equals 7.

See solution 79.

Here is the intelligence test which the Roman general Publius Quintilius Varus, in the year 9 A.D., gave to his legionnaires in order to choose a commander. The instructions were to continue the following sequences of figures, adding one number to each. As smart as he was, Varus nevertheless lost the battle in the Teutoburger Forest and committed suicide. Can you pass this test?

See solution 137.

See solution 53.

See solution 138.

See solution 56.

See solution 54.

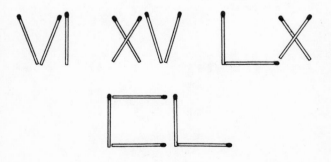

See solution 86.

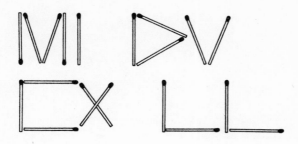

See solution 50.

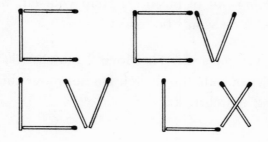

See solution 87.

13. Clearance Sale

Come in! Come in! Come to our big clearance sale! We are going out of business! Help yourself, while the stock lasts! You won't be sorry!

A coin lies on a shovel. Move 2 matchsticks so that the coin lies outside the shovel. Do not move the coin or the other 2 matchsticks.

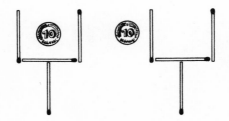

See solution 106.

Here are 2 equilateral triangles. Take away 3 matchsticks and add 2 so that you still have 2 equilateral triangles.

See solution 112.

With 10 matchsticks, construct 4 deltoids in the shape of a 4-pointed star. Do not bend or break any of the matchsticks.
See solution 103.

With 6 matchsticks, lay out 2 deltoids which do *not* have a side in common. Again, do not bend (or break) any of the matchsticks.
See solution 133.

Can you lay out 6 matchsticks on the table so that every matchstick touches all the others?

See solution 150.

Lay out an island with 4 matchsticks and a pool around it with 12 matchsticks. With the island placed as shown in the drawing, with a one-matchstick separation, the "water" around it cannot be bridged with a *one*-matchstick bridge. This is because the bridging match must be supported at both ends; since the separation is a full matchstick-length, the "bridge" would float otherwise.

However, you can build a stable bridge with 2 matchsticks. How?

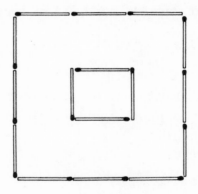

See solution 115.

How can you lift a whole pile of matchsticks with only 1 additional matchstick?

See solution 73.

Lay out a row of 8 matchsticks. Put the first 4 match-sticks heads up, the second 4 heads down. Now rearrange

this row in 4 moves so that the matchsticks stand alternately head up and head down—that is, the first should be head up, the second head down, the third head up, and so on. In doing this, always take 2 side-by-

side matchsticks with 1 move and lay them down in another place. Also, do not turn any of the matchsticks upside down.

See solution 135.

Can you construct a square using 2 matchsticks, without bending or breaking them? And, can you also make a triangle with 1 matchstick, also without bending or breaking it?

See solution 55.

Build a coin bank on a tablecloth using 4 matchsticks. Place a coin in the safe. How can you get the coin out of the bank without touching the coin or the safe?

See solution 42.

Can you, now, without a support of any kind, lay out 3 matchsticks on a table so that their heads do not touch the table? Can you do this same trick with 4 or 6 matchsticks?
See solution 136.

Can you balance 13 matchsticks on one single matchstick? This is not a trick, like solution *73* was, but it is an actual physical miracle!

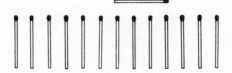

See solution 120.

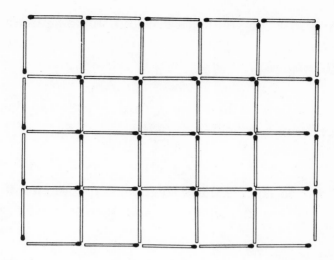

Remove 12 matchsticks from this figure so that 2 squares of the same size and 6 six-sided figures of the same size result.

See solution 60.

If you take away 16 matchsticks from the same figure, can you end up with 1 square and 4 same-sized six-sided figures?

See solution 75.

Set aside 12 matchsticks and pretend that each matchstick is exactly 1 yard (metre) long. In each of the following problems, use all 12 matchsticks.

How can you fence in 9 square yards (metres) with them?

See solution 41.

And how can you fence in 8, 7, 6 and 5 square yards (metres)?

See solution 51.

Can you fence in 6 square yards (metres) so that the fence forms a triangle?

See solution 151.

Can you change this triangular shape into a different form so that it contains 5 and then 4 square yards (metres)?

See solution 62.

Finally, how can you surround 3 square yards (metres) with the 12 matchsticks?

See solution 34.

Here is a problem that many great mathematicians have tried to solve:

First, lay out 10 matchsticks. Out of these, construct 5 crosses, one after the other. To make these crosses, you must use 1 matchstick at a time to jump over no more

or less than 2 others. An already constructed cross counts as 2 matchsticks. Are there several solutions?
See solution 63.

The Bridge

Place 2 matchboxes on the table so that they are separated by a space slightly greater than the length of a matchstick. Can you build a stable bridge from box to box with only 4 matchsticks?

See solution 45.

Pi

The famous number pi ($\pi = 3.14159265\ldots$) indicates how many times larger the circumference of a circle is than its diameter or its area greater than the square of its radius. The precise value of pi cannot be expressed by a whole-number fraction (in which the numerator and the denominator are both whole numbers). There is, however, a whole series of rather simple fractions whose values come astonishingly close. In the following problem, a sufficiently approximate value is 3.14. After you know that, you can easily solve the problem.

Move 1 matchstick so this equation becomes equal on both sides.

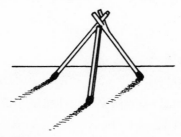

See solution 89.

Pyramid

Wedge 2 matchsticks together and support them with a third so that a pyramid results. Can you lift the matchsticks up with a fourth match?

See solution 153.

Puzzling it Out

Here's the last bit of stock remaining in the "puzzling" clearance sale. Each player gets 3 matchsticks and, without the others seeing, holds in his or her closed hand any number of them from 0 to 3. Each player then lays his or her fist on the table. Taking turns, each person guesses how many matchsticks there are altogether in the fists on the table. If someone guesses the number exactly, he or she drops out of the game. The matchsticks are then reshuffled, and a new round begins. Whoever stays to the end of the game loses and pays a forfeit.

14. The Solutions

1. 8 less

9 less

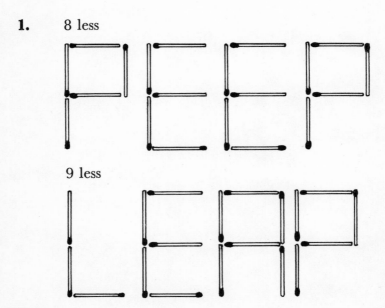

10 less

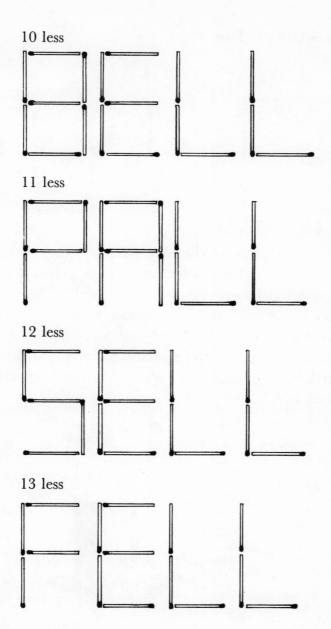

11 less

12 less

13 less

2. Answers b, c, d and e are correct.

3.   **4.**

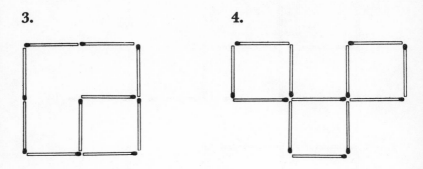

5. Take the sleeve of the matchbox between your lips and set it down on top of the matchsticks. Inhale deeply. The matchsticks will hang on as if glued to the end of the sleeve because inhaling creates a partial vacuum and air pressure presses the matchsticks against the opening. Now move the matchsticks over the drawer of the box and exhale to break the vacuum and release the matchsticks.

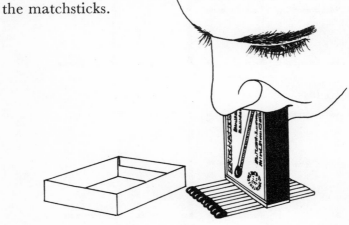

6.

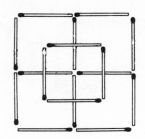

7.

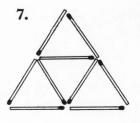

8.

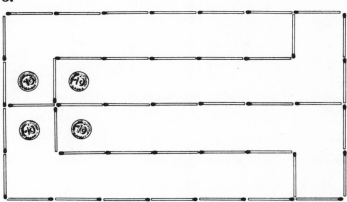

9.

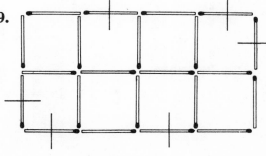

10.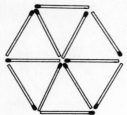

11.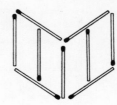

12.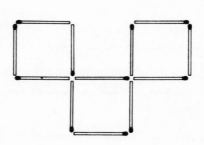

13.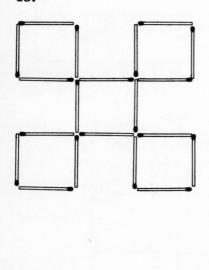

14.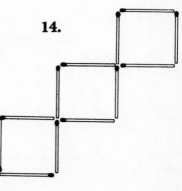

15.

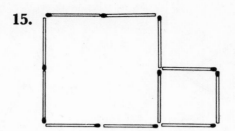

16.

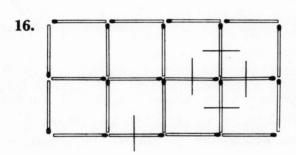

17.

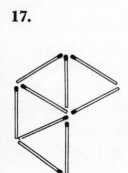

18.

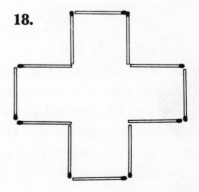

19.

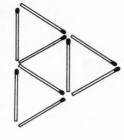

20.

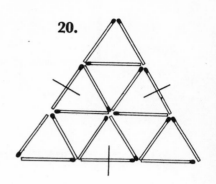

21. Trixor used a box which contained 17 matchsticks. On the bottom, he wrote: "You will choose 3 matchsticks," but he carefully hid the writing at first. During the performance, Trixor took 10 matchsticks out of the box, leaving only 7 in it. He placed the pile of 3 matchsticks closer to the player than the other pile. When the player chose that pile, which usually happens, Trixor turned the box over and showed the written prediction. If the player had chosen the other pile, Trixor would have said, "See, I knew you would choose the pile with 7 matchsticks in it—there are also 7 matchsticks in my box!" In this case, of course, the writing on the bottom of the box was not revealed. When you perform this trick, be careful not to repeat it for the same people.

22.

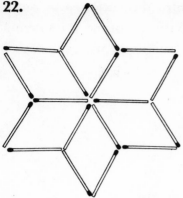

23.

take away 1 equals

24. 12 ones + 6 fours + 2 nines = 20 triangles.

25.

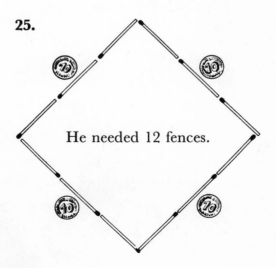

He needed 12 fences.

26. The solution lies in the third dimension. Lay out a triangle with 3 matchsticks. With the other 3, construct a pyramid over it to make 4 equilateral triangles whose sides are 1 matchstick long.

27. Whoever can take the sixth matchstick wins. The opponent then takes 1, 2 or 3 matchsticks from the remaining 5. This leaves the first player 3, 2 or 1 to take away and win.

28.

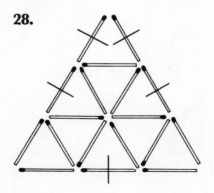

29.

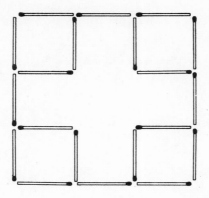

30. To prepare for this trick, Trixor broke off a match-stick and jammed it crosswise into the box with the head still on it. This prevented all the other match-sticks from falling out. Over these held-down match-sticks, he placed 1 loose matchstick to use at the beginning of the demonstration. He then removed the shortened matchstick—making sure, however, not to show that it was only a half—and the other matchsticks were free again.

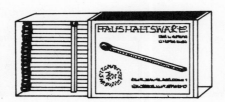

31.

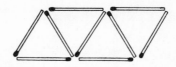

32. The area is $1\frac{1}{2}$ times $18 = 27$.

$3 \times 3 = 9.$ $3 \times 3 = 9$ $3 \times 3 = 9$

33. When, after one turn, a player succeeds in leaving 9 matchsticks lying on the table, and then later at least 5 matchsticks, he will never lose.

34.

35. To do this trick, Trixor hid a short length of wooden stick or dowel (a) in his hand. When closing the box, he secretly stuck the dowel into the drawer (b). When he pulled the string at both ends, the box stood still (c). When he opened the box to let the children check it, he removed the dowel and hid it.

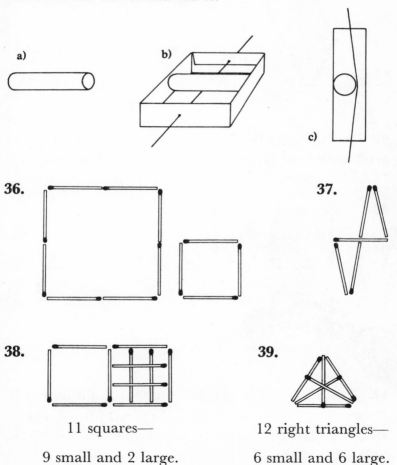

a)

b)

c)

36.

37.

38.

11 squares—

9 small and 2 large.

39.

12 right triangles—

6 small and 6 large.

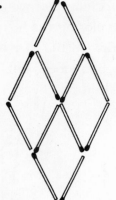

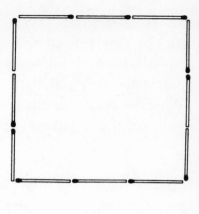

42. On the open side of the "safe," scratch on the table-cloth with your fingernail until the coin slides out.

43.

44. This is not a solution, but only a helpful hint. Try solving the problem once more, thinking: Must a square always be bordered only by matchstick *lengths*? If you still get nowhere, *see solution 109.*

45. Here is how to interlock the 4 matchsticks to make the bridge.

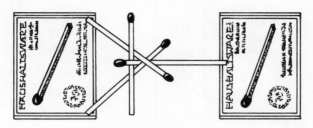

46. The magic handkerchief actually consisted of 2 same-sized handkerchiefs which were carefully sewn together around the edges. Between them was an empty matchbox (box B). Box A, which was the one that disappeared, was covered with the cloth. The magician reached his right hand under the handkerchief (as if arranging it) and took box A. At the same time, his left hand took hold of box B and lifted it up under his helper's nose. While the helper took box B in his hand, the magician stuffed box A away unnoticed in his pocket. Practice this in front of a mirror before you perform it!

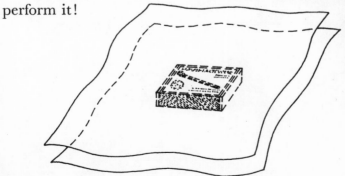

47.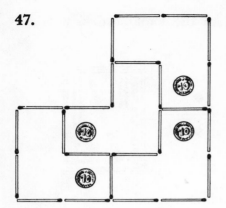

48.

Lay down 5 matchsticks, take away (the number) 8, nothing is left.

49.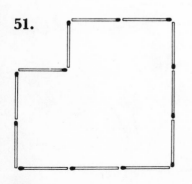

50.

On the left, write the next lower figure; on the right, write the next higher figure.

51.

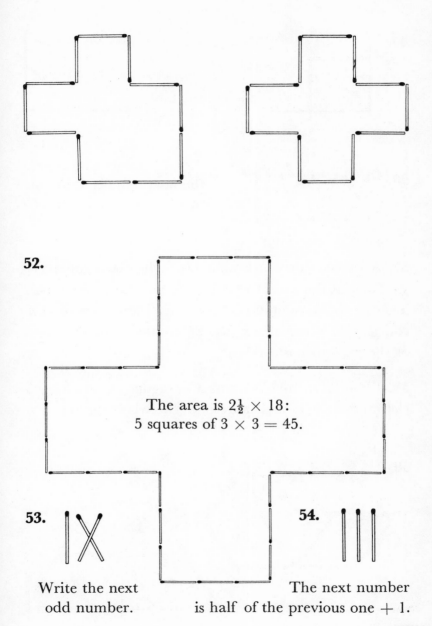

52.

The area is $2\frac{1}{2} \times 18$:
5 squares of $3 \times 3 = 45$.

53.

Write the next
odd number.

54.

The next number
is half of the previous one + 1.

55.

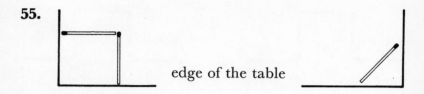

edge of the table

56. 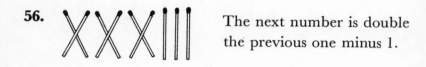   The next number is double the previous one minus 1.

57. A player can win if after his or her own turns 21, 16, 11 or, at the least, 6 matchsticks remain on the table. This is also true if the player must start second. Of course, if the first player also knows the secret trick, he or she can win instead!

58. 1 rhombus (middle) and 3 hexagons—2 small ones (left and right) and 1 large one (the whole figure).

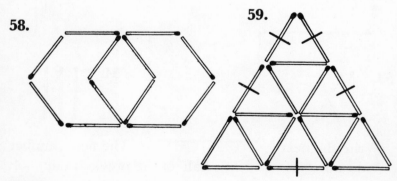

58.

59.

60.

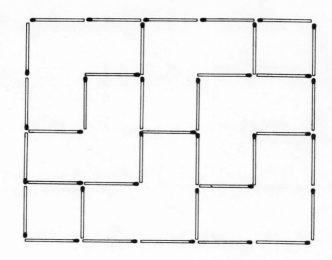

61.

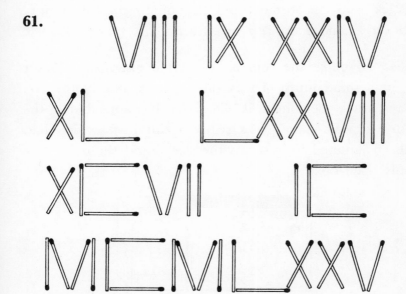

62.

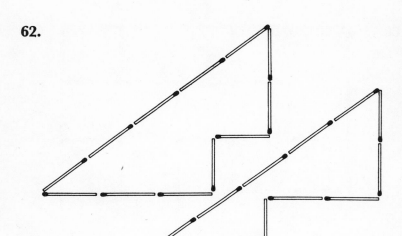

63. One mathematician discovered 24 original and 24 mirror-image solutions. Two of these are: move matchstick 5 on top of matchstick 2, 7 on 10, 3 on 8, 9 on 6, 1 on 4; and 4 on 1, 7 on 3, 5 on 9, 6 on 2, 10 on 8.

64. To make the coin on the table disappear, Trixor put a small lump of wax on the underside of the box and stuck the coin to it. The coin that appeared in the drawer of the box was really a duplicate which had been jammed in between the sleeve and the drawer of the open box.

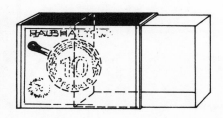

Trixor closed the box by giving it a powerful slap. This loosened the coin and also covered the noise it made when it fell.

65.

66.

67.

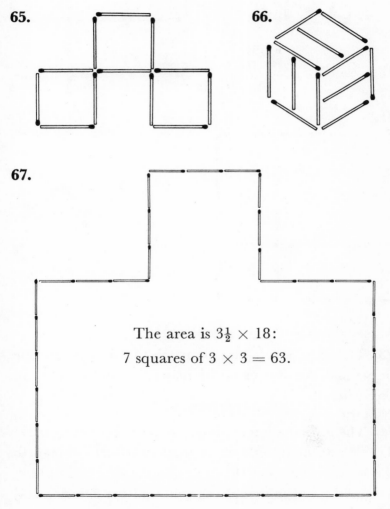

The area is $3\frac{1}{2} \times 18$:
7 squares of $3 \times 3 = 63$.

68. Answer e is correct.

69. **70.**

71.

72.

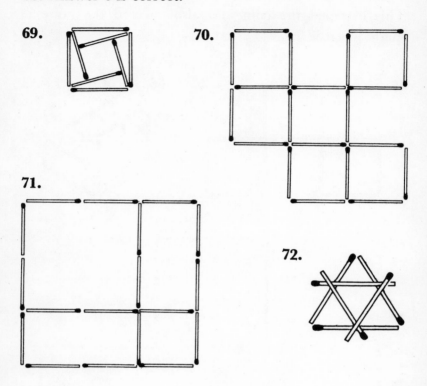

73. This is a joke: Jam a matchstick inbetween the sleeve and the drawer of the matchbox and lift the full box with it.

74. The explanation is easy. In setting up the trick, Trixor attached a 30-cm. (1-foot) long black thread to the sleeve of the box. When he slid the drawer in place, he made sure the thread went around the entering end

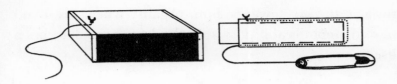

of it. On the other end of the thread, he put a safety pin which he also attached to the lining of his trousers pocket.

In performing the magic trick, Trixor put the box on the back of his hand and moved his hand slowly and unnoticeably forward. He thus created the impression that the box was moving by itself towards him. When he turned his hand over, he placed the thread between his index and middle fingers, so that when he slowly moved his hand, the box appeared to move towards

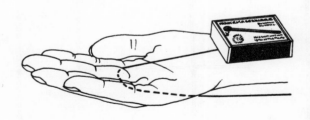

his fingertips. Finally, Trixor stood the box on end on his palm and held it firmly. The thread was on the surface turned towards him. Again, when his hand moved unnoticeably forward, the box seemed to open itself.

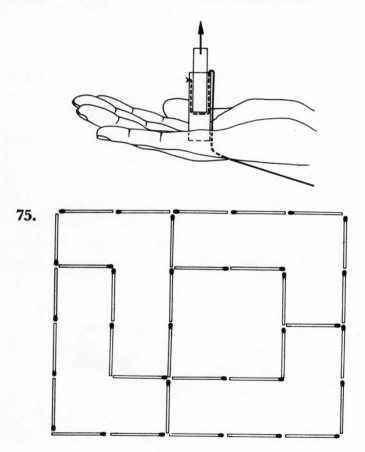

75.

76. Trixor brought the matchstick under the cloth with his left hand. Under the cloth, he held it firmly between his palm and the base of his thumb. Then he stretched all his fingers out straight, took hold of the second match-stick—it was hidden in the seam of his necktie—and lifted it up. The assistant held and then broke the matchstick.

Trixor released the palmed match while shaking out the cloth.

77.

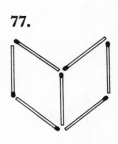

78. This is how 8 goats were enclosed with 22 fences.

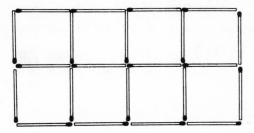

79. This is a joke: Half of 12 (in Roman numerals) is 7. The top part of the drawing looks normal; the bottom looks like a mirror image.

80.

The area is $4\frac{1}{2} \times 18$:
$9 \times 9 = 81.$

81. He began counting clockwise at the matchstick marked with an X.

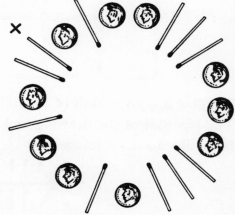

82.

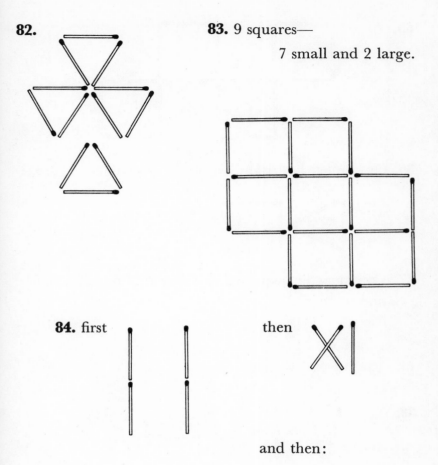

83. 9 squares—

7 small and 2 large.

84. first   then   and then:

The magician had 10 matchsticks hidden in his pocket. While the first 3 parts of the trick were being laid out, he secretly and unnoticeably took out the extra 10 matchsticks and hid them in his hand. He then picked up the last matchstick, shook it between his hands and—11 matchsticks fell on the table!

85.

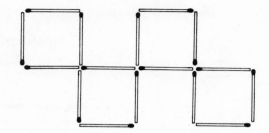

86. On the left and right, write the next higher figure.

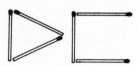

87. Continue the sequence as follows: $+5$, -50, $+5$ . . . and so on.

88.

89.

$22 \div 7 = \text{pi}$

90.

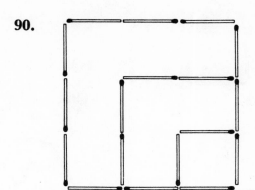

91.

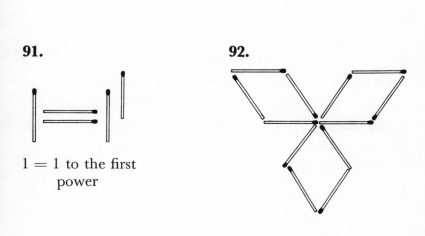

$1 = 1$ to the first power

92.

93.

$1 =$ square root of 1

94.

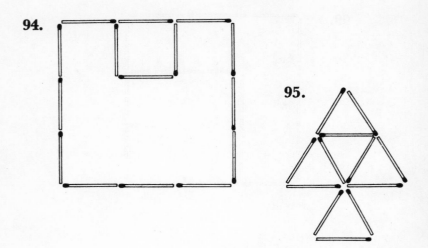

95.

96. Lightly blowing the matchsticks together produces the seeming magnetism. This is one of the finest table tricks when it is well practiced and correctly performed. Be sure to do it only once, or someone from the audience might catch on.

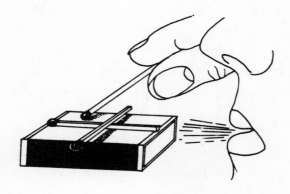

97.

98. For this trick, the matchbox must be prepared beforehand. Using water, remove the label from a second box and glue it to the bottom of the first one. Now, nobody can tell which is the top and which the bottom. Cut out the bottom of the box drawer and glue the matchsticks to it. Glue or paste white paper to the sides of the drawer to strengthen them. The (cut-out) bottom can fall back and forth but cannot slip out past the sides.

Place the drawer in the sleeve with the glued-on matchsticks facing up. Put a loose matchstick on top of them. This matchstick is the one to show the audience. When you turn the box over, the bottom of the drawer falls downwards. When you open the box again, the drawer seems to be empty.

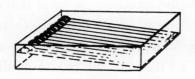

99.

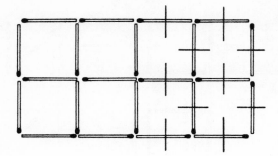

100. 2 rhombuses and 5 rhomboids—4 small and 1 large:

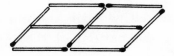

101. A player wins when, on the last draw, the opponent has 7 matchsticks to choose from. If the opponent previously had 28, 21, or 14 matchsticks to choose from, the player can also win.

102. The matchstick pierced exactly through its middle was prepared beforehand by twisting it back and forth, so that it moved easily around the pin's shaft. When the magician snapped his finger against the matchstick, it only seemed to go through the pin. Actually, he quickly turned the safety pin around 180° in the other direction. Thus, the magic was really an optical illusion, unnoticeable because the matchstick's head was missing.

103.

104.

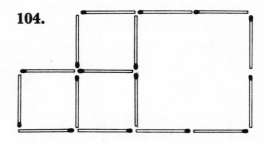

105. The somersault takes place by means of a snap of the magician's fingernail. When you perform this trick, be sure to hold the second matchstick near its head

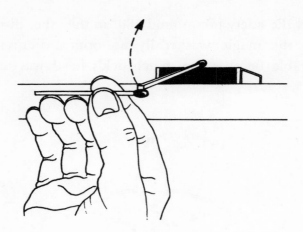

between your thumb and forefinger. Place your middle finger lightly against the matchstick. Hold your hand with the palm turned up.

Now, raise the projecting end of the first matchstick slightly and snap the nail of your middle finger very lightly against the second matchstick. . . .

Simple and effective though this trick may be, you must practice it well.

106.

Starting figure,   move one,   move another one.

107.

108.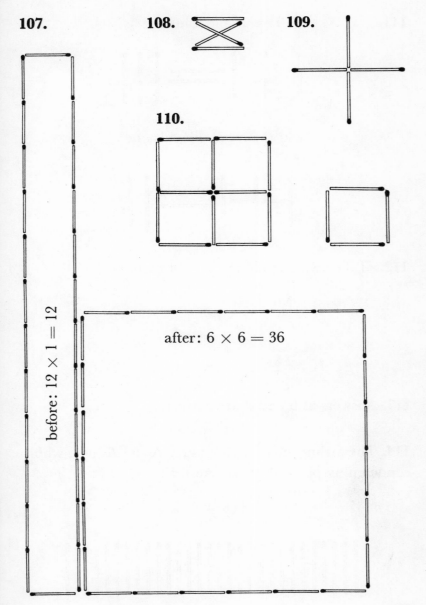

109.

110.

before: $12 \times 1 = 12$

after: $6 \times 6 = 36$

111. The simple solution:

and the more difficult one:

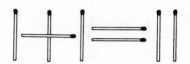

112. Take away 3 and add 2, 1 of them broken.

113. Answers a, b and d are correct.

114. The arrangement saving party A (heads up), while condemning party B, looks like this:

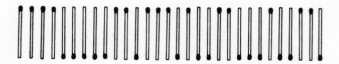

You can memorize the sequence of heads-up-heads-down matchsticks with these nonsense phrases: *"You mean I am a deer? I say, yes, dear."* Assign the vowels in the sentences the following values: a = 1, e = 2, i = 3, o = 4, and u = 5. Thus, you begin with 4 matchsticks heads up, then 5 heads down, and so on.

115. Place one matchstick across the corner of the bank, and the other from this matchstick to the corner of the island to make the bridge.

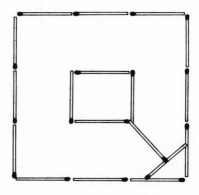

116. 11 squares—8 small and 3 large.

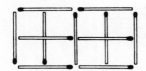

117.

118.

119.

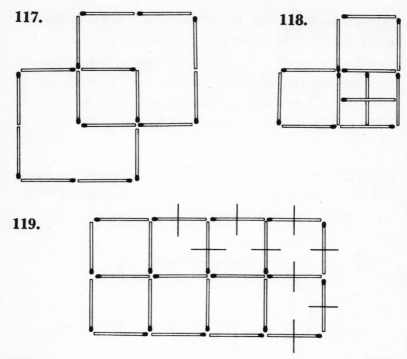

120. On 1 matchstick, place the other 12, alternating the heads right and left as shown. Put the 14th matchstick across and on top of the 12 matchsticks, parallel with the first one. Then lift the 13 matchsticks on top with the 1 matchstick underneath.

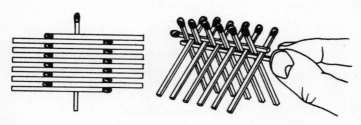

121.

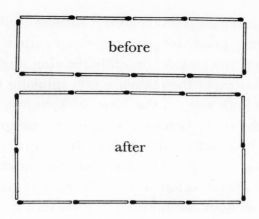

before

after

122. Here again, there is no solution, but only a small hint. How many dimensions are there? Try once more to solve the problem yourself. If you still cannot solve it, then *see solution 26*.

123. One surface of each of 2 matchsticks had a large dot made of black construction paper. At first, the matchsticks were held downwards at about the height of the upper thigh, with the clean sides towards the audience. Then, the matchsticks were quickly raised to about shoulder height. While doing this, at about breast height, the magician turned the matchsticks over—during the upwards movement—with the tips of his thumb and index finger.

131

The whole trick is based on this turning of the matchsticks—they must be turned either when moving upwards or downwards, or while the ring finger covers a side. This tricks the audience into thinking that they have seen both sides of the matchstick empty.

This fine trick, however, is also an example of the fact that it is not enough just to know the trick. You must spend a long time practicing the movements in front of a mirror before you perform it. If you present the trick without the necessary practice, a fiasco could result and your entire audience could catch on to the trick!

124.

125.

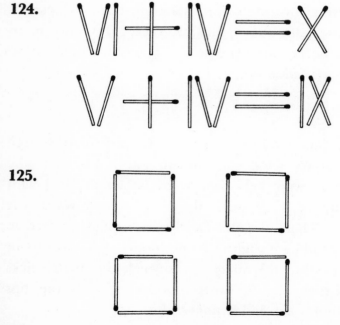

126. This is a fascinating and puzzling trick whose secret must not be revealed. The magician sat with the left side of his body turned towards the audience. Three times, the magician's hand formed an arc from his hairline to his assistant's hand. Twice, the matchstick actually touched the hand of the assistant. On the third rise of his hand, the magician quickly and without being observed, thrust the matchstick into his hair. Without stopping, he then struck his helper's hand for the third time, but with his outstretched index finger instead of the matchstick. At first, the magician simply left the matchstick in his hair. Later, he unobtrusively removed it.

127.

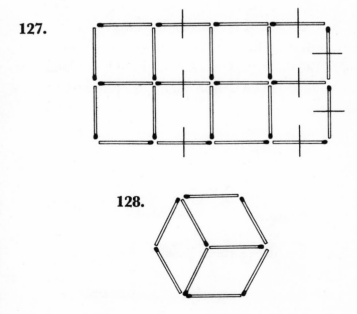

128.

129.

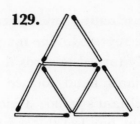

130. Unnoticed, the magician shoved a piece of rubber tubing about 1.5 cm. (about ⅝ inch) long over the ends of the matchsticks. In this way, he could easily move the matchsticks. During the performance, his fingers covered the rubber. Afterwards, he handed the hair over for examination first. As someone from the audience reached for the hair, the magician pulled the matchsticks out of the rubber tube and also released them for examination.

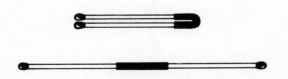

131. The winning player must remove the matchsticks so that 2 piles with an equal number of matchsticks always remain for the opponent (5 + 5, 4 + 4, 3 + 3, 2 + 2). At the position 2 + 2, the opponent takes 1 or 2 and the winning player then takes 2 or 1.

132. The farmer can dispense with 6 more fences, and then the pen would look like this:

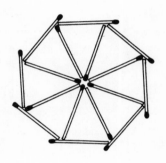

133.

134.

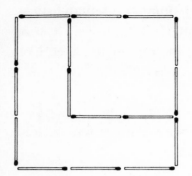 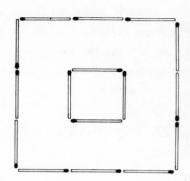

135. Starting position: first move:

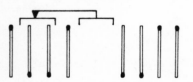 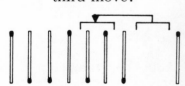

second move: third move:

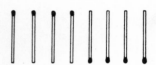 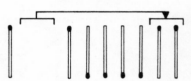

fourth move:

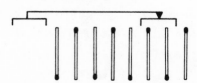

136.

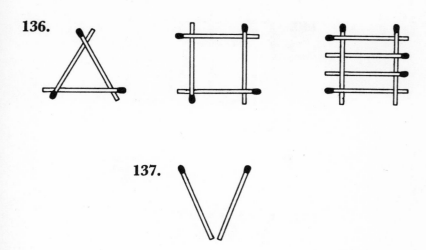

137.

138. Continue the sequence with multiples of 4.

139. The magician's wand was made of black cardboard, and the ends were decorated with white paper. In one end of the tube, Trixor placed some soft soap, in the other end, a piece of sugar cube. The grease from the soap spreads out in the water and causes the matchsticks to float towards the edge of the bowl. The sugar draws the water and the matchsticks back to the middle again.

140.

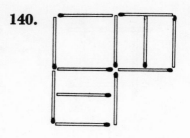

141.

$\frac{3}{4}$ dozen = 9 matchsticks.

If you move the matchsticks, you can make 3 dozen (the Roman numeral 36).

142.

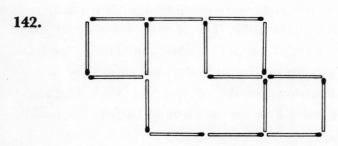

143.

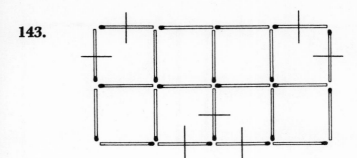

144. A rubber band was fastened to the middle of the bottom of the sleeve of the matchbox and was then attached to the front and back of the bottom part of the matchbox drawer. When the drawer was pushed outwards and the fingers pressed against the sleeve, the box remained open. Releasing the finger pressure made the box close by itself.

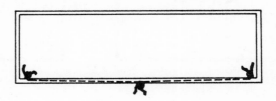

145.

146.

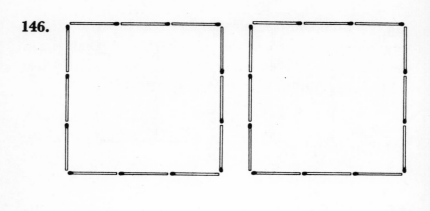

147.

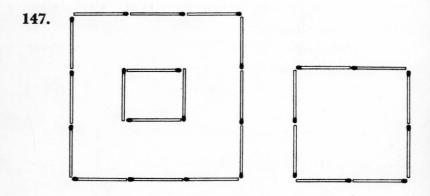

148. The secret of the old magician is simple. The answer *always* comes out 18 if the total of the digits of any number of matchsticks between 20 and 29 is subtracted from the original number chosen. Also, at the beginning of the trick, the full chest (matchbox) must be filled with 36 coins (matchsticks). Then the brothers will always end up with the same inheritance.

149. The happy pig:

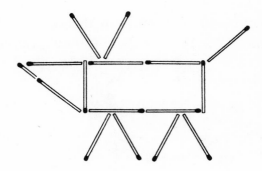

150. Each matchstick touches the other 5 at the same time.

151. The area of a triangle:

$$\frac{a \times b}{2} = \frac{3 \times 4}{2} = \frac{12}{2} = 6$$

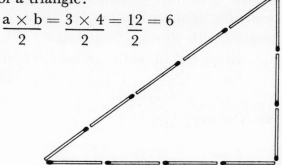

152. Ibrahim adds his camel to the rest, so there are 40 altogether. The first son gets 20 (half), the second 10

(a fourth), the third 5 (an eighth), and the fourth 4 (a tenth). One camel is left over and the wise man rides away on it.

153. Reach the fourth matchstick under the pyramid, so it somewhat supports the 2 wedged matchsticks, until the third pyramid matchstick falls on the fourth. Drop the wedged matchsticks a little again, until the end of the third matchstick projects under the place where the matchsticks are wedged together. You can now raise the other 3 matchsticks with the fourth one.

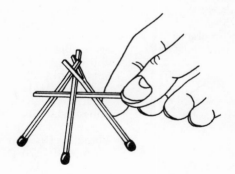

Index